CW01079809

Corridors of Flour

Corridors of Flour

ISBN 978-1-9163145-9-7

First published in Great Britain in 2021 by
The Conservative and Unionist Party
4 Matthew Parker Street
London
SW1H 9HQ

Cover cartoon by Paul Thatcher

Typeset in American Typewriter and Strawberry Blossom

Printed in Great Britain by Paragon Customer Communications

Introduction

Turn on the hob. Heat up that oven. Prepare those pots and pans. For the first time in more than thirty years, the Conservative Party has published a cookbook.

Councillors, activists, MPs and Peers have shared their favourite recipes just for you. From Amanda Milling's Staffordshire Oatcakes to Oliver Dowden's Jammy Steamed Sponge, there's enough variety for even the pickiest of eaters.

We've also managed to get a few former Prime Ministers on board. So why not try David Cameron's Italian pasta, followed by Theresa May's scones? A meal fit for a king — or two Prime Ministers.

Finally, if you're looking for a midnight snack, Boris Johnson has shared his method for grilling the perfect cheese on toast — and it's probably the only time in history a snack has been personally approved by the Prime Minister.

But enough appetisers. It's time to move on to the main course. We hope you'll enjoy making these recipes. And if you feel particularly inspired, why not share your results with us on social media? Just use the hashtag #ConservativeRecipes.

Bon appétit!

Savoury

Soups, lasagnes, pastas and pizzas
— if you eat it, we've got a recipe
for it. WARNING: if you weren't
feeling hungry before, you will
after looking through this section!

Cheese on Toast

– The Rt Hon. Boris Johnson MP, Uxbridge and South Ruislip –
Prime Minister and
Leader of the Conservative Party

Cut a large amount of cheese,
preferably Cheddar, into slices.

—

Lightly toast some brown bread.

—

Spread toast with butter and chutney.

—

Cover toast with slices of cheese.

—

Grill until it gets all nice and golden.

For best results keep grilling until the edges of the
cheese have turned brown and perforated and are
faintly scabby in appearance and texture.

—

Eat quickly before you are caught.

I just love making yummy homemade soups and you can make so many from just one base which makes it so quick and easy to do whilst also relatively healthy and filling.

My 'Soup for Starters Recipe' is great for those looking to make soup for the first time or even have a go at using different flavours or making different types of soup to try.

Soup for Starters

- Amanda Solloway MP, Derby North -

30 minutes

Depends on the volume of ingredients

Ingredients:

Olive oil

Chopped onions

Chopped garlic (according to taste)

Stock cube (according to type of soup)

Water

Wine of choice (if you are feeling extravagant!)

Cream (if desired)

Seasonings of your choice

For the main ingredients try whatever combination you prefer e.g. carrot and coriander, ham and leak, tomato and basil (I have chosen mushroom soup!)

Method:

1: Warm oil in a saucepan and then add onions, fry until onions going clear.

2: Add all other ingredients and warm through for a couple of minutes, stirring frequently.

3: Add stock cube of choice and as much water to give you your desired thickness/texture.

4: Bring to boil and then simmer.

5: Blend until smooth (if desired).

6: Season to taste and serve.

When I was growing up my mother Adele regularly made a wonderful vegetable soup or vegetable broth especially during the winter. It brings back many childhood memories for me and a few years ago I asked her to teach me how to make it myself. The precise ingredients can be changed to meet an individual's taste but broadly speaking this is how I do it.

Vegetable Soup

- The Rt Hon. George Eustice MP, Camborne and Redruth -

30 minutes

1-2 people

Ingredients:

1-2 carrots finely chopped

2 small potatoes chopped into small cubes

A couple slices of swede

½ onion finely chopped

1 green cabbage chopped finely

750ml vegetable stock

40-50g butter

Method:

1: Take a good chunk of butter (about 40-50 grams) and put it in a large saucepan.

2: Add the carrots, potatoes, swede, and onions but not the cabbage. Simmer the vegetables in pan of melted butter on a medium to low heat stirring regularly for about 8-10 minutes.

3: Next take 750ml of dissolved vegetable stock. I usually use Bouillon powder. Put 3 good teaspoons into 750ml of boiling water. After the vegetables have gently simmered for 8-10 minutes in the melted butter only add the vegetable stock and stir in.

4: Simmer the liquid mixture for a further 10-12 minutes on a medium heat stirring every few minutes.

5: Then at the very end add the chopped-up cabbage and simmer for a further 2-3 minutes. It is important not to add the cabbage too early or it will discolour the whole broth and the cabbage will be over-cooked.

6: Allow the broth to stand and cool slightly for 10 minutes and then it is ready to eat.

Leek and Potato Soup

- Caroline Nokes MP, Romsey and Southampton North -

45 minutes

2-3 people

Ingredients:

4 leeks
2 medium potatoes peeled and diced
1 medium onion chopped
50g butter
850ml chicken stock
275ml milk
A pinch of salt and pepper

Method:

1: Trim the tops and roots of the leeks, split in half lengthways and slice finely. Wash under cold running water and drain well.

2: Use a large thick based saucepan to melt the butter then add leeks, potatoes and onion stirring well. Season with salt and pepper and cover – leave to sweat over a low heat for 15 mins.

3: Add the stock and milk bring heat up to simmering point. Place the lid back on the saucepan and simmer for 20 mins.

4: Blend the mixture well, return to the heat and reheat gently then it's ready to serve.

This is an easy soup with only 6 ingredients, using healthy "superfood" vegetables which are in season at the same time and available from the local farm shops in Cheshire. My family call it "Pink Soup" and my three daughters love the tangy, sweet flavour. We eat it hot, but it could equally be eaten cold and is delicious with a chunk of crispy sourdough bread. Enjoy!

Beetroot and Rhubarb Soup

– Edward Timpson CBE MP, Eddisbury –

40 minutes plus 1 hour roasting time

6 people

Ingredients:

500g each of rhubarb and beetroot
1ltr chicken or veg stock
Generous knob of butter
Black pepper to taste
Crème fraîche to serve

Method:

1: Peel beetroot, cut into even pieces, cover and roast at 180°C for about an hour.

2: Roughly chop rhubarb and fry in butter till soft.

3: Add the cooked beetroot.

4: Add enough stock to cover the vegetables.

5: Bring to the boil and simmer for 20/25 minutes until the vegetables are just soft.

6: Whizz with a hand-blender till smooth.

7: Add black pepper to taste and swirl in a little crème fraîche.

Gibraltar Gazpacho

- Henry Smith MP, Crawley -

10 minutes

2 people

VEGAN

This delicious cool summer soup is healthy, vegan and a favourite of mine whenever I visit Gibraltar or indeed Spain.

Ingredients:

1 tbsp white wine vinegar

30g white bread – torn into pieces

1 red pepper – seeded and diced

½ peeled cucumber – sliced into chunks

300g large tomatoes (halved and seeded)

150g baby tomatoes

½ red chilli – seeded and sliced into quarters

½ red onion – peeled and diced

1 small garlic clove – peeled

A handful of fresh thyme leaves – chopped

100g ice cubes

A few drops Tabasco sauce

2 tsp extra virgin olive oil – to serve

Method:

1: In a small bowl, mix the vinegar with 50ml cold water and ½ tsp salt. Put the bread in the vinegar mix to soak and set aside.

2: Meanwhile, put the pepper, most of the cucumber, the large and baby vine tomatoes, chilli, onion, garlic, and most of the thyme leaves in a blender. Add the soaked bread, the ice, and the Tabasco (if using) and blend until smooth. If you prefer a chunkier soup, blitz briefly in a food processor. Season to taste.

3: Serve between 2 bowls. Chop the 6 remaining baby tomatoes and scatter over the soup. Top with the remaining chopped thyme and cucumber, a drizzle of olive oil and a grinding of black pepper.

It is 7am. Just come in from the dawn raid on a rainy election day. Cold, wet, tired but most importantly hungry. What could be a better way to boost your energy than the Dawn Raid Breakfast

Loaf! A hollowed-out loaf of bread with layers of hash browns, bacon, sausages, beans and topped off with egg. A perfect way to reenergise for the remaining campaigning sessions.

Dawn Raid Breakfast Loaf

- Tom Mobbs, President of Nottingham University Conservative Association -

20-30 minutes

2-4 people

Ingredients:

1 loaf of unsliced bread
6 sausages
8 rashers of bacon
1 tin of baked beans
10 hash browns
A knob of butter
3 eggs
200g grated cheese

Method:

1: Cook sausages, bacon, beans, and hash browns as stated on packaging.
2: Hollow out the loaf of bread.
3: Heat up butter and glaze the inside of the loaf.
4: Cook loaf (unfilled) for 5 mins on 180°C.
5: Fill the loaf with the rest of the food, crack the eggs on top of the loaf (Order: hash browns, sausage, beans, bacon, beans, sausage, hash browns, cheese, eggs).
6: Continue in the oven for 15 mins.

Quick, simple, and delicious. After a long day of university work, Welsh Rarebit is a go-to meal before heading out into Cardiff City Centre. As either breakfast, lunch, or dinner, it is the perfect meal to slot into any busy schedule: whether that be from exams or campaigns.

Welsh Rarebit

- Joe Kidd, Cardiff University Conservative Society -

15 minutes

2 people

Ingredients:

250g grated mature
Cheddar cheese

20g butter

2 tbsp beer

1.5 tbsp
Worcestershire sauce

1 tsp English mustard

Black pepper

4 slices white bread

Method:

1. Lightly toast the bread.
2. Heat the butter in a pan until melted. Mix together the butter, grated cheese, beer, Worcestershire sauce, and English mustard. Stirring until combined, season with black pepper.
3. Spread a layer of the mixture over each slice of toast, ensuring it covers the crusts too.
4. Place each slice of toast onto a baking tray and place directly underneath the grill for roughly five minutes, until golden brown and bubbling.
5. Remove from the oven, cut each slice in half and serve hot.

Garlic Focaccia

- Dean Russell MP, Watford -

1 hour

3-4 people

Ingredients:

250g strong white bread flour
175ml warm water
1 tsp table salt
5 tbsp olive oil
1 sachet dried active yeast
A pinch sea salt
A pinch fresh rosemary

Method:

1: In a small pot, crush 2 cloves garlic and add 3tbsp olive oil to infuse it with the garlic (to make fresh garlic oil). Stir then close the lid and shake. Wait 5 minutes.

2: In a large bowl, add the flour, yeast, salt and 1tbsp garlic oil and then gradually add the water. You may not need all of it, but you may need more.

3: Mix the dough until it comes together.

4: Tip out onto a floured surface and knead for 10 minutes or until it is a smooth and elastic dough.

5: Onto the surface pour 1tbsp garlic oil and roll out to a generous thickness.

6: Place onto lined baking tray and scatter rosemary, sea salt, 2 cloves finely chopped garlic and the remaining garlic oil.

7: Cover with cling film and prove for 15-20 minutes. During this time preheat oven to 220°C, Fan 200°C.

8: Once risen bake the focaccia for 12-15 minutes or until golden brown.

Ingredients:

500g strong white flour, plus extra for dusting

2 tsp salt

1 tsp dried yeast

3 tbsp a good quality oil or 30g softened butter

300ml tepid milk or water

1 large egg

12 black olives

A handful of Cheddar cheese

Olive And Cheese Bread

- Dirk Russell, Area Campaign Manager, Hampshire, IOW and Surrey -

3 hours

2-4 people

Method:

1: Mix 500g strong white flour, 2 tsp salt and the tsp of yeast in a large bowl.

2: Make a well in the centre, then add 3 tbsp olive oil and 300ml milk and egg. Mix well. If the dough seems a little stiff, add another 1-2 tbsp milk and mix well.

3: Tip onto a lightly floured work surface and knead for around 10 mins.

4: Once the dough is satin-smooth, place it in a lightly oiled bowl and cover with cling film. Leave, in a warm room, to rise for 1-2 hours until doubled in size.

5: Line a baking tray with butter. Knock back the dough (punch the air out and pull the dough in on itself). Flatten the dough and evenly add the cheese and olives. Fold the dough over to form a shape to fit your baking tray. Leave the dough in the baking tray for 40 minutes until doubled in size.

Do not leave for over long as the dough will receive too much air and drop back before baking.

6: Pre-heat oven to Fan 170°C. Dust the loaf with some extra flour. Bake for 40 mins until golden brown and the loaf sounds hollow when tapped underneath. Cool on a wire rack. Alternatively, at Step 5 cut the dough into 8 even segments. Flatten each segment and add the cheese and olives. Fold over the dough until you make a ball-like shape. Put your roles onto floured parchment paper and cover with a tea towel. Let the balls prove from 40 minutes to an hour in warm place. Place into a warm oven and bake for 20 minutes.

There is nothing better than a Sunday roast with your nearest and dearest. But what, friends, is a roast without Yorkshire puddings? A sad, emaciated, shadow of the glory it is meant to be. And this, ladies and gentlemen, is not just any Yorkshire pudding, but a Stilton Yorkshire pudding. I use the wonderful creamy, tangy Stilton from either Cropwell Bishop or Colston Bassett dairies in Rushcliffe, Stilton making at its finest!

Stilton Yorkshires

- Ruth Edwards MP, Rushcliffe -

30 minutes
to 1 hour

2-4
people

Ingredients:

250g plain flour

¼ tsp salt

150ml milk

150ml cold water

4 beaten eggs

100-200g crumbled Stilton
(depending on taste)

1 tbsp chopped fresh
herbs, either use chives or
parsley

Method:

1: Sift the flour into a bowl and add the salt.

2: Combine the milk and water in a jug.

3: Make a well in the middle of the flour and add the beaten eggs and water.

4: Pour in a little of the milk and water mixture and whisk together to make a smooth batter. Mix in the rest of the liquid until you have a batter the consistency of single cream.

5: Leave the batter to stand for 15 minutes, meanwhile pre-heat the oven to 230°C, Gas 8.

6: Now comes the moment to add the herbs and stir in the Stilton, add between 100-200g depending on your taste.

7: Grease a Yorkshire pudding or muffin tin and leave to heat in the oven for 10 minutes.

8: Carefully remove the tin and pour in the batter, return to the oven, and cook for 15-20 minutes – do not be tempted to open the door before they are risen and bronzed, or they will sink into the abyss.

You can, of course, vary the ingredients for the filling to suit vegetarians by substituting the minced beef with finely chopped carrots and, say, cauliflower, lentils/chickpeas and up the quantity of onions, potato, and garlic. Also, substitute the beef stock cube for a veggie one.

The finished pasties are best stored, once fully cooled, in a airtight tub in the fridge and can last up to 2-3 days for a greedy family of four (such as ours), I prefer to reheat them in the oven (best not to microwave them as the pastry goes soggy). For parties I like to serve them warm as large canapés with an ice-cold beer or shandy. As they say in Malaysia – Makan Suip! Come and get it...

Alina's Curry Puffs

– Simon Baynes MP, Clwyd South –

3
hours

4–6
people

This recipe has been passed down my wife Maggie's family from her mother, Alina, who grew up in Malaysia. The curry puffs are delicious either hot or cold and, for us, bring back many happy memories of family meals. I am indebted to Maggie for these detailed recipe instructions.

Ingredients:

Filling:

Two 400g packs minced beef (20% or more fat gives it taste) or 800g finely chopped chicken (breast or thigh) or veg

4 medium potatoes – floury – the type that absorb flavour, chopped into small cubes

2 tablespoons of curry paste from a jar. You can vary this for spiciness. But this quantity is just right for spice addicts and phobes alike.

2 large onions, finely chopped

6 large cloves garlic, finely chopped

Half teaspoon turmeric powder

One beef stock cube (per 400g pack of mince): I like the stock pots – nice flavour. Change to chicken or veggie depending on preference.

1 generous squirt each of tomato paste and tomato ketchup

Salt and pepper to taste (at the end of cooking)

Olive oil/sunflower oil a few tablespoons for frying

(be generous – the diet starts tomorrow)

The Pastry:

One 400g pack ready-made shortcrust pastry

Plus, one 400g pack ready-made puff pastry

One beaten egg (or milk for veggie option) to glaze the puffs before baking

A few dustings of plain flour for rolling the pastry

Alina's Curry Puffs

– Simon Baynes MP, Clwyd South –

Method:

The filling

1: Fry the onions and garlic gently with a pinch of salt and some oil, stirring until the onions are translucent.

2: Throw in the curry paste and fry for a minute.

3: Add tomato paste, ketchup, and minced beef, stir well and fry till brown.

4: Add stock cube(s), a cup of water and simmer on low heat until the potatoes are ready to add from another pan.

5: While the mince is cooking, parboil for about 10 minutes the cubed potatoes in a separate pan with turmeric powder and salt added to the water.

6: Stir the parboiled and drained potatoes into the curried mince and simmer in a gentle oven 150°C for 1-2 hours to let some of the liquid evaporate. Be careful that it doesn't dry out though.

7: Once the filling is cooked, stir in salt and pepper to taste, leave to cool and then overnight in the fridge (curry always tastes much better the next day plus it's easier to fill the pastry cases when the filling mixture is still cool).

Alina's Curry Puffs

- Simon Baynes MP, Clwyd South -

Filling the pastry cases (Next Day):

8: This bit takes time so you may want to get friends and family involved...

The tried and tested magic to this pastry is a combination of the two; the flaky gives enough fat to melt in your mouth without being too greasy and the shortcrust ensures the curry puff holds its shape. So, to start, roll out both shortcrust and flaky pastry once placed on top of each other. Cut into four squarish sections and keep layering and rolling each section so each is well combined. Take each section and roll out to cut about 6 pastry cases with a glass or pastry cutter. (Once you've cut all your cases, use the remaining pastry to make more cases). Finally roll each case to as thin as you dare (3-4mm works for me), fill each one as you would a mini pasty, wetting one side edge of the inside semicircle with water to seal. Press the sides together and, for a professional look (as well as a leakproof edge), crimp the edges. You may need to watch how to do this on YouTube, but it is oh-so-satisfying when you succeed. It took me many hours to master the technique as I'm left-handed and usually quite hopeless at such things. Lay about 6, well-spaced, on a greased baking sheet, brush the top and edges with beaten egg and bake for about twenty minutes in a fan oven at 175°C. You will smell when they are ready but if you can investigate the oven, the pastry should be a golden sandy colour rather than brown. Cool them on a tray and, if possible, eat as soon as you can.

Ingredients:

2 cans of green / young jackfruit (in water or brine, not syrup)

1 onion diced

2 garlic cloves crushed

1 tsp cumin

1 tsp chilli powder

Flakes of Jalapeño peppers or chilli flakes to taste

250ml vegetable stock

8 tortilla wraps

Barbecue Sauce

250g tomato passata

2 tbsps apple cider vinegar

2 tbsps maple syrup

1 tbsp soy sauce

1 tsp ground cumin

A pinch of salt and pepper

I have been vegetarian since I was young, and there are certainly more meat substitutes available now than when I was growing up. One of my favourite alternatives to meat is jackfruit, which is becoming more popular and much easier to find.

Most of the big supermarkets stock it and you can pick it up in any Asian grocery shop. Jackfruit soaks up flavour, and when shredded its consistency means it bears more than a passing resemblance to pulled pork!

Pulled "No Pork" Burritos

- The Rt Hon. The Baroness Sugg CBE -

1
hour

4–6
people

Method:

1: Drain the jackfruit and rinse. If it is in brine, rinse a few times and press to fully drain.

2: In a large frying pan or wok, heat up some olive oil and sauté the onion for about 10 minutes until browned, adding the garlic with a few minutes to go.

3: Add the rinsed jackfruit and the spices. Add diced jalapeños or chilli flakes to taste. Mix to combine then add the vegetable broth.

4: Bring to a boil and then turn down to simmer. Cook for 10-15 minutes, stirring occasionally, until all the liquid is gone.

5: Pre-heat the oven to 200°C. Whilst the jackfruit is cooking, prepare the barbecue sauce. Mix all the ingredients in a saucepan and simmer for 10 minutes, until slightly thickened. When the jackfruit is cooked, shred it by using two forks pulling in the opposite direction.

6: Pour the BBQ sauce over the shredded jackfruit, stir through, then spread evenly onto a baking tray. Bake for 15 to 20 minutes, which browns and dries the mixture making it the perfect consistency to use and eat!

7: Place into a tortilla and wrap into a burrito, adding sliced avocado, grated cheese, or coleslaw as you wish. Can be re-heated in the oven or wrapped in foil and put on the BBQ.

Recipe Tip

Divide the risotto between two bowls and serve with a good dry white wine.

Ingredients:

150g Arborio or Carnaroli rice

2 or 3 chicken thighs

2 crushed cloves of garlic

1 litre chicken stock

50 – 75g broken walnut pieces

100ml dry vermouth

30-50g salted English butter

A sprinkle Granda Padano / Parmesan

A dash of truffle oil

A handful of dried lemon thyme

A pinch of salt and pepper

Chicken Risotto

- Chris Clarkson MP, Heywood and Middleton -

30 minutes

2 people

Method:

1: Start by heating a wide-based non-stick pan to a medium-high heat then add half the butter and all the crushed garlic – watch the temperature, you do not want the butter to brown as it will lead to an overpowering, bitter taste.

2: Chop the chicken into medium sized chunks and begin frying off in the butter and garlic.

3: Once the chicken is browning, add in the remaining butter, rice, and begin moving it around the pan with a good wooden spoon or a non-stick spatula, do not let it sit in any one place for too long. Once the rice is coated, add in the broken walnut pieces, and continue to stir.

4: At this stage, if you are on an electric/halogen hob, turn the heat to a medium setting and pour in half the vermouth. If you are on gas, pour in the vermouth and slowly lower the temperature until roughly half the vermouth has evaporated – continue to stir the mixture vigorously. Stirring releases starch from the rice which will give you a nice creamy texture at the end.

5: Once the mixture is starting to take on a sticky complexion, pour in the remaining vermouth and continue to stir until the rice has absorbed most of it. Continue to stir throughout.

6: Now begin to add stock slowly, enough to cover the rice each time, stirring throughout. When the stock levels have reduced below the rice, add more and continue to stir. This should take 15-20 minutes. When you come to add the last stock, add in the thyme, and continue to stir until you can smell the herbs.

7: When the rice mixture is thickly sticky (enough to stick to your spatula or spoon) and the remaining stock has been absorbed, take the risotto off the heat, and allow to sit for around a minute. This ensures the dish will remain sticky and glutinous.

8: Finally, add a good dusting of Grana Padano, a hearty drizzle of truffle oil, a quick dusting of black pepper and salt and optionally, finely sliced black truffle (not essential, but gives a lovely mouthfeel), and stir the mixture thoroughly one last time.

Courgette Chicken Pasta Dish

- Daisy Campbell, Conservative Student -

20 minutes

5 people

Ingredients:

3 courgettes

3 onions

1 packet of pancetta

2 cloves of garlic

5 chicken breasts

A handful grated cheese

1 tbsp oil

A handful mixed herbs

500g pasta

1 tbsp cream cheese

Method:

1: Cook the chicken in the oven for the recommended time, sprinkle mixed herbs on top.

2: Chop the onion and cook in a tablespoon of oil until golden.

3: Grate the courgette and add to the onions to cook.

4: Add the cream cheese to melt in with the courgette and onions.

5: Separately cook the pancetta and add to mixture.

6: Cook the pasta.

7: Once chicken is cooked, chop up and merge everything together to complete the dish.

This is a super easy and delicious dish that Samantha and I often cook at home. Inspired by the *River Café Cook Book*, this is our family's own simplified twist on an old classic. It's a favourite of all the family.

Italian Sausage Meat Pasta

- The Rt Hon. David Cameron -
Prime Minister, May 2010 to July 2016

35 minutes (approx.)

4 people

Ingredients:

2 red onions

6 spicy Italian sausages

Handful rosemary

Splash red wine

2 tins chopped plum tomatoes

Parmesan cheese

500g pasta (preferably penne)

½ pint double cream

Method:

1: Fry 2 chopped red onions in a large, deep frying pan. Add the meat squeezed from 6 spicy Italian sausages. Throw in the chopped rosemary and red chilli.

2: Turn up the heat and break up the sausage. Once the meat has been broken up and browned, add a splash of red wine and reduce. Then add 2 tins of chopped plum tomatoes.

3: Reduce the sauce, as with Bolognese. Grate loads of Parmesan in a bowl. Once the pasta (preferably penne) is ready, add together with the Parmesan, ½ pint of double cream and the sauce.

I first had crab pasta in a tiny restaurant in Venice when I visited the city for a Council of Europe meeting. Crab is a great British ingredient and makes a special flavour from a very simple recipe. It's very flexible, so you can easily add more chilli, garlic and seasoning to suit your taste. My children love it and with a side salad and some garlic bread it makes a good family meal, maybe with a dry white wine to accompany.

Crab Pasta

- David Simmonds CBE MP, Ruislip, Northwood and Pinner -

Sauce 5 minutes,
plus pasta
cooking time

4
people

Ingredients:

100g fresh crab meat, mixed white
and brown

½ tsp dried chilli flakes
(or more if you prefer it quite spicy)

3 tbsp olive oil

4-5 cloves fresh garlic

If available, some chopped fresh
parsley or wild garlic leaves are
a tasty garnish

Method:

1: Crush and chop the garlic and
soften it in the olive oil over a
very low heat, along with the chilli
flakes. It is important not to brown
the garlic, so best to cook it gently
for about four minutes.

2: Add the crab meat and mix
thoroughly then take off the heat.
The sauce is made.

3: Combine with your choice of cooked
pasta and scatter parsley, wild
garlic, or black pepper if you wish.

Recipe Tip

Serve in big bowls (preferably with some garlic bread) and enjoy!

Ingredients:

250g dried macaroni

200g mild cheese either mozzarella or gouda

100g grated or chopped stronger cheese

600ml semi skimmed milk

150ml double cream

75g butter

75g plain flour

2 rashers of smoked bacon

2 cloves of garlic, finely chopped

1 packet of "Wotsits" or other cheese puffs

A sprinkle of salt and pepper

I wholeheartedly believe there is no food more comforting than mac and cheese. It has long been one of my favourites for cold autumn nights curled up in front of the TV. The best thing about mac and cheese is its versatility. You can use a huge range of different cheeses and add all kinds of extra fillings to make it your own. I used to be a "cheese sauce from a jar" kind of girl but, during lockdown, I taught myself the art of the cheese sauce.

Bacon-and-Wotsit-Topped Mac and Cheese
- Dehenna Davison MP, Bishop Auckland -

45 minutes

3-4 people

Method:

1: Pre-heat the oven to 200°C. In a medium saucepan, boil the water then add the macaroni. Leave to simmer on a medium heat. Cook according to packet instructions – but leave a little al dente as it will continue to cook in the cheese sauce.

2: Whilst the macaroni cooks, chop the bacon into small pieces then fry in a lightly oiled pan. Cook until brown and crispy – it should only take a few minutes – then transfer to a sheet of kitchen roll to drain any oil. When cooked, remove the pasta from the heat and drain.

3: In a large saucepan, melt the butter over a medium-low heat. Gradually stir in sieved flour to make a roux. Slowly stir in the milk. It may initially look lumpy, but keep at it, adding the milk slowly. Then slowly stir in the cream for extra richness. By now, the texture should be pourable but thick.

4: If desired, add the chopped garlic. I find it adds a great bit of flavour to the sauce. Gradually add the grated cheese and stir until melted. Then add salt and pepper for taste.

5: If you feel the sauce is too thin, you can add some extra cheese, or a little extra sieved flour. But be careful – with flour, it can thicken very quickly. Take the cheese sauce off the heat and set aside. Get the drained bacon and chop into small, crumb-like pieces.

6: Whilst still in the packet, crush the Wotsits or cheese puffs until they are a small, breadcrumb-like size. Add the macaroni into the cheese sauce and stir well until it is fully and evenly coated, then pour into an oven dish.

7: Add both the bacon and Wotsit crumb on top in an even layer. If you prefer, you can use breadcrumbs and parmesan cheese. Bake in the centre of the oven for 20-30 mins until golden brown on top. I prefer to slightly overbake so the cheese sauce around the edge gets nice and crispy.

VEGETARIAN

Vegetarian Lasagne

- Ben Houchen, Tees Valley Mayor -

45 minutes

2-4 people

Ingredients:

500g Quorn mince

3 tbsp olive oil

1 onion, finely chopped

3 cloves of crushed garlic

150g mushrooms, chopped

200ml water

2 tins chopped tomatoes

3 tbsp vegetarian red pesto

1 vegetable stock cube

Sprinkle salt and freshly ground black pepper

8-10 lasagne sheets

25g butter or margarine

25g plain flour

300ml milk

200g mature Cheddar cheese, grated plus extra for topping

Method:

1: Preheat the oven to 200°C.

2: Heat the oil in a frying pan and fry the onion and garlic for 5 minutes until softened.

3: Add the mushrooms and cook for a few minutes.

4: Stir in the Quorn mince for 3-4 minutes.

5: Add the tomatoes, vegetarian red pesto, vegetable stock cube and the water. Increase the heat and simmer gently for 5 minutes.

6: Make the white sauce by melting the butter, stir in the flour and cook gently for a minute stirring constantly. Slowly add the milk and reheat until beginning to thicken. Add the cheese, season and simmer for 3 minutes.

7: Spoon half of the mince mixture over the base of an ovenproof dish, top with lasagne sheets, add white sauce, repeat the layers, then pour over rest of the cheese sauce and scatter with cheese and bake in the oven for 20 minutes until the top is golden brown.

8: Serve immediately with garlic bread.

There is just something about this dish that feels comforting - it never fails to perk me up and is good all year round!

Sundried Tomato and Basil Risotto

- Elliot Colburn MP, Carshalton and Wallington -

30 minutes

2-4 people

Ingredients:

3 tbsp butter

1 large onion

2 cloves of garlic

100g sundried tomatoes

220g risotto rice

A splash of dry white wine

800-1ltr of vegetable stock

As much as required of Parmesan

A pinch of salt and pepper

A handful of fresh basil

Method:

1: Heat the butter in a saucepan until melted. Add the onion and garlic and fry gently for a few minutes until soft. Add the rice, fry for a minute. If you are using the wine, pour in and stir over a medium heat until mostly absorbed. Then stir in a bit of the stock until it has almost all been absorbed, and keep repeating, gradually adding stock until the risotto is cooked al dente.

2: Meanwhile, tip the sundried tomatoes and a splash of boiling water into a liquidizer and blend until smooth. Add to the risotto mixture and cook for a further 2-3 minutes.

3: Remove from the heat and stir in your preferred amount of parmesan and season to taste. Spoon into a bowl, top with fresh basil and a you can even grate a little more cheese on top, then dig in!

Ingredients:

For the gluten-free base

400g gluten free bread flour

2 tsp golden caster sugar

2 tsp gluten free baking powder

1 tsp fine salt

5 tbsp olive oil
Xanthan gum

For the sauce and topping

2 tbsp olive oil

1 small onion – finely chopped

One 400g can of chopped tomatoes

2 tbsp tomato puree

1 tsp caster sugar

½ small bunch of basil leaves – shredded

Two 125g balls of buffalo mozzarella

As someone with coeliac disease, I miss enjoying the meals I used to be able to eat before. However, this gluten-free homemade pizza recipe tastes just like normal pizza and it's super easy to make whilst at university as it cooks in just 10 minutes. I picked pizza as it's the best thing to enjoy after a night at Port and Policy!

Gluten-free Homemade Pizza

- Emily Preston, Conservative Student -

24 hours to rest the dough plus 50 minutes

2-4 people

Method:

1: Heat the oven to 220°C, Fan 200°C, Gas 7 and put two baking sheets inside.

2: Make the sauce: heat the oil in a small saucepan and cook the onion with a generous pinch of salt for 10 mins over a low heat until softened. Add the chopped tomatoes, purée and sugar and bring to a gentle simmer. Cook, uncovered, for 25 – 30 mins or until reduced and thick, stirring regularly. Blitz the sauce with a hand blender until smooth. Season to taste and stir through the basil. Allow to cool a little.

3: Make the dough: mix the flour, sugar, baking powder, salt and xanthan gum in a large mixing bowl. Make a well in the centre and pour in 250ml warm water and the olive oil. Combine quickly with your hands, to create a thick, wet, paste-like texture, adding an extra 20ml warm water if the dough feels a little dry. Store in an airtight container or covered bowl in the fridge for up to 24 hours before using. Lightly flour two more baking sheets. Split the dough into two and flatten with your fingers into 20 – 25cm rounds on the sheets.

4: Finish the bases with a thin layer of the sauce and torn up mozzarella. Place the baking sheets on top of the hot baking sheets in the oven and cook for 8-10 mins or until crisp around the edges.

VEGAN

Vegan Cottage Pie

- The Rt Hon. Esther McVey MP, Tatton -

**45 minutes
-1 hour**

**4
people**

Ingredients:

2 onions chopped

2/3 leaks finely sliced

5 carrots chopped

1 stick of celery finely chopped

1 clove of garlic crushed or very finely chopped

1 x tin of tomatoes (400g)

1 x jar of tomato sauce or crushed tomatoes

2 x 400g tins of green lentils

1 packet of chilli paste

1 tsp of dried rosemary

1 tsp oregano

1 vegetable stock cube

6 regular potatoes

5 sweet Potatoes

Method:

1: Put small amount of vegetable oil in a large pan and sweat the vegetables down until the carrots are soft approx. 15 mins. Add a splash of white wine and bring to the boil.

2: Then add both the tomatoes, tomato sauce, green lentils and other ingredients as required and cook slowly on the hob for another 15 minutes.

3: Then put in the oven for 15 minutes with tin foil on top so as not to dry out.

4: Finally – into a cup squeeze the juice of ½ lemon, crush a clove of garlic and add a dessert spoon of olive oil and sprinkle this across the top of the potato topping. Leave in the oven on a high heat until the potato slightly crispy to touch.

To dampen the spicy side of the dish, I sometimes add sweetcorn to the jollof rice after it is fully cooked and cooled down. I then mix it in. It adds an extra flavour to an already tasty dish.

Ingredients:

4 tbsp of canola/vegetable/sunflower oil
1 tbsp of butter
4 fresh tomatoes
1 6oz can of tomato paste
4 red onions
2 red bell peppers
1 – 2 scotch bonnet
4½ cups of long grain parboiled rice
2 x cups of chicken stock

Spices required:

A sprinkle of stock cube
A sprinkle of bay leaves
A sprinkle of curry powder
A sprinkle of garlic or onion powder
A sprinkle of ginger

Other ingredients:

A pinch of salt
A handful of thyme leaves

The essence of this famous West African dish is the base or sauce. No Nigerian, Ghanaian, Ivorian or Senegalese wedding, naming ceremony etc. is complete without some jollof rice. Each country has some slight variations to how they make theirs but all taste fabulous.

Jollof Rice

- Festus Akinbusoye, Police and Crime Commissioner for Bedfordshire -

1 hour 40 minutes

4-6 people

Method:

1: Soak rice in a container with warm water.

2: While rice is soaking, heat about 4 tablespoons of oil and butter in a medium-sized pot on medium heat and throw in some chopped red onions. Allow the onions to fry until the redness starts to slightly fade off.

3: Next, add tomato paste and let it fry with the onions. Make sure to stir the paste consistently to avoid burning. Do this for about 10 mins, or until the paste fully fries in the oil. Add in your optional crayfish for an extra tasty flavour.

4: Blend some tomatoes, onions, scotch bonnet and red bell peppers together until you achieve a smooth consistency. You can add some water to this if too thick. Pour in the blended mixture into the pot and fry it together with the tomato paste and onions.

5: Add all your spices (but do not salt yet) and mix. Cover the pot and allow the tomato to fry in the oil. Add more oil if necessary. You really want to let the tomato fry to remove the slappy sour taste, so make sure you do not rush this process. I would recommend letting it fry for about 20-30 mins. Be sure to continuously stir the mixture to avoid burning.

6: At this point, while the tomato base/sauce is frying, begin to rinse out the rice. Make sure to get rid of as much starch as possible by washing the rice until the water used becomes clear. This helps to prevent the rice from sticking together when cooking. Once the tomato is done frying, add your chicken stock to the mix and taste to see if it requires any salt. Add salt if necessary and mix.

7: Now add in your washed rice (and a bit of water if necessary to cook the rice) and mix it together with the fried tomatoes. Turn down the heat to the lowest on your burner and cover the pot. I personally like to cover the pot with aluminium foil before putting on the lid just to make sure the heat stays within the pot without escaping from the lid hole.

8: Allow the rice to cook for about 30 minutes. It might be necessary to stir the rice to avoid it burning at bottom of the pot. After about 30 minutes open the pot and properly stir all the ingredients together. Cover the pot again, and let it cook for an additional 10 minutes or until the rice has fully blended in with the mixture.

Quick, healthy, and fresh but, importantly, only use white meaty fish (Cod/Halibut) from a sustainable source. Serve with mashed potato, green salad or fresh steamed green vegetables.

Creamy White Fish with Capers

- Rebecca Pow MP, Taunton Deane -

15 minutes

4 people

Ingredients:

4 white fish steaks
(from a sustainable source)
300ml single cream
2 tbsp capers
1 lemon
Salt and pepper to taste

Method:

1: Fry steaks in a little olive oil for 5 minutes on each side

2: Add cream and simmer for a few moments ensuring the fish is cooked through.

3: Add capers, salt and pepper

4: Squeeze of lemon juice

A perfect Saturday night autumn/winter supper, this is an adaptation of the 70s dish Chicken Divan. I have adapted it from my best friend's mum's recipe and it always tastes different and always very tasty.

It a warming, comforting mild curry dish which is quite like a hot coronation chicken with a cheesy crispy crisp top. YUM!

I don't think of the calories.

Saturday Night Chicken Diva

- Mims Davies MP, Mid Sussex -

1 hour

2-3 or 4-6 people
(depending on the
chicken quantity)

Ingredients:

2 or 4 free range chicken breasts or diced pieces

1 large broccoli crown

1 tin of vegetable soup or chicken and vegetable soup

Mayonnaise, to taste

Curry powder (or curry paste korma or tikka depending on your preference), to taste

1-2 stock cubes – vegetable or chicken

Squeeze of lemon juice from store cupboard if you have it

For the topping

One pack of grated cheese

2/3 packets of plain crisps – I use Pom bears!

Method:

1: Poach the chicken for 20 mins in the stock – until no pink meat. Put the oven on to warm.

2: Blanche the broccoli for 4 mins – drain and leave aside.

3: Meanwhile heat the oven to around Fan 180°C.

4: Pop the soup into a large casserole bowl, add the blanched broccoli, with several tablespoons of mayonnaise plus the curry power, lemon juice and warm for 10 mins.

5: Add the diced chicken breast any additional mayonnaise or curry power depending how spicy you like things and how thick you want the sauce, plus black pepper. Add the grated cheese on top and mix in the crushed crisps.

6: Cook till golden brown, usually at least another 15/20 mins.

7: Serve with basmati rice and or jacket potato with a side of peas.

Ingredients:
50g butter
A big splash olive oil
2 chopped onions
125g sliced bacon/pancetta
4 sliced garlic cloves
8 chicken pieces – thighs or breast
250g sliced mushrooms
500ml Riesling / dry white wine
250ml cream
A sprinkle of salt and pepper
A handful of chopped parsley

This is amazing comfort food. Takes no time and great for a dinner party. You can have it with new potatoes, or dauphinois, to help mop up the delicious creamy mushroom sauce.

Amazing Chicken in a White Wine, Cream Sauce

- Guy Opperman MP, Hexham -

45 minutes

4-6 people

Method:

1: Melt the butter and oil together in a large pan.

2: Brown the chicken pieces (5 minutes front and back should suffice) and remove from the pan.

3: Add the onions and bacon and allow to fry until the onions are soft and translucent and the bacon has rendered its fat.

4: Add the garlic and allow to sauté for another 30 seconds before removing the mixture from the pan (leaving the fat behind).

5: Add the mushrooms and allow to fry for 5 minutes.

6: Add the onion and bacon mixture along with the browned chicken back to the pan.

7: Pour in the wine and allow to come up to a boil. Turn down the heat and cover. Allow to simmer until the chicken is cooked through. This should be 10-15 minutes

8: After a max of 15 minutes, uncover, turn up the heat and add the cream. Allow to cook gently for another 5-10 minutes. Add the chopped parsley and season to taste.

Recipe Tip

Curry paste, tamarind, and stock make anything taste good, which makes this the perfect recipe for a busy minister. The vegans among us can swap out the fish for pressed tofu which takes on the flavour beautifully – I still prefer salmon though.

I have been making this recipe with my father since I was young. In fact, it was while making curry that he told me countless stories of why he's wanted to leave the EEC since he was 15.

Manic Minister's Thai Fish Curry

- Joseph Reeve, YC Chair for High Wycombe -

30 minutes

2 people

Ingredients:

2 salmon fillets
(pressed tofu works well too)

1-2 tbsp Thai red curry paste

1-2 tbsp lemongrass / 1 lemongrass stalk chopped

1-2 tbsp tamarind paste

½ a fish stock cube + 200ml water

1 tbsp fish sauce

400g green beans

1 whole lime squeezed

250g cherry tomatoes, halved

1 handful chopped coriander

2 servings white rice

Method:

1: Prep and start cooking rice to be ready in 10 minutes. Add red Thai curry paste, fish stock, fish sauce, tamarind, lemongrass to a saucepan – bring to the boil and simmer.

2: Trim beans and chop in half, add to saucepan. Bring to boil and simmer for 5 minutes.

3: Chop salmon into bite sized lumps (remove skin). Squeeze half lime juice onto the salmon. Add fish and tomatoes to the pan. Bring to boil and simmer for 5 minutes. Add remaining lime and coriander.

4: Serve on rice.

Recipe Tip

Serve with pancakes, hoisin sauce, spring onions, shredded and finely sliced cucumber pieces or Jasmine Rice.

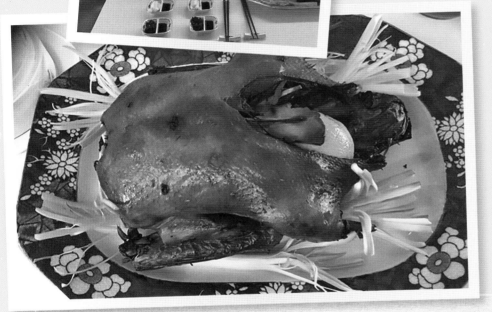

Ingredients:

2kg oven ready duck

5 shallots – peeled and chopped

1 litre chicken stock

400ml light soy sauce

300ml chinese rice wine

3 tbsp clear honey

3 star anise

3 pieces fresh ginger

1 zest of an orange

1 spicy vegetable oil for brushing

Years gone by, I used to hang the duck to dry out once I had washed it, as this was the way I was directed by the cooks at the Good Earth Restaurant in Kings Road Chelsea, a frequent haunt back in the 70's.

I decided there must be a better way to cook my favourite dish so after many tries, came up with this solution which ensures the duck was totally devoured by all and thoroughly enjoyed.

Aromatic Peking Crispy Duck

- Lesley Taylor, Conservatives Abroad -

3 hours

2-4 people

Method:

1: Place the duck breast side down in a colander in the sink.

2: Boil a full kettle of water then pour inside and over the duck giving it a drenching. Then leave the duck to drain so that the water evaporates.

3: Place the shallots, soy sauce, Chinese rice wine, star anise, honey, ginger pieces, orange zest, and pinch of salt in a litre of chicken stock in a saucepan/wok in which the duck will sit tightly and bring to a gentle roll.

4: When the required roll has been reached, carefully place the duck, breast side down into the broth which should almost cover the duck, cover with lid, and allow to poach gently for about 2 hours. Turn the duck over for the last 30 minutes to complete the braising. Whilst cooking, shred the spring onions for later.

5: Remove the duck from the broth, by inserting a wooden spoon into duck and gently lifting on to a wire rack to drain.

6: Strain the broth for later or if not going to eat, then freeze. Rest the duck in a cool place to dry for a few hours before completing the roasting. If preferred, store covered in the fridge to roast the following day. Set the oven to 200°C, Fan 180°C, Gas 6.

7: Allow the duck to come to room temperature, then brush spicy vegetable oil over the duck and place on a rack in a roasting tray in the oven for 30 –40 minutes to allow the skin to become crispy and a glossy deep brown.

Ingredients:
4 tbsp natural yogurt
1 tbsp turmeric
1 tsp salt
4 small lamb shanks
2 tbsp sunflower oil
4 onions – two white
– two red sliced
A jar of madras curry paste
8 garlic cloves chopped
40mm piece ginger, grated
1 tin of chopped tomatoes
1 tsp dried chilli flakes
4 cardamom pods, split
3 tbsp lime pickle
400ml chicken stock

This is a warming dish that can only be described as proper comfort food.
It requires a fair amount of preparation, but pretty much cooks itself once you've
done your prep. Enjoy!

Lamb Shank Curry

- Marcus Jones MP, Nuneaton -

3 hours **4 people**

Method:

1: Mix the yogurt, cumin, turmeric, 1 tsp sea salt in a large mixing bowl, then add the lamb and coat it with the mixture. Pop in the fridge for a couple of hours to marinate.

2: Once the lamb shanks have marinated. Pre-heat an oven to 160°C, Fan 140°C, Gas 4. Heat the oil in a large heavy bottom casserole pot, use medium heat and add the lamb and brown all over for 10 mins, then remove from the pot and set aside. Add the onions to the pot and fry for 10 minutes or so until they are soft. Stir in the madras paste, garlic and ginger and cook for 2 mins.

3: Add the tomatoes, chillies, cardamom pods and lime pickle, give it a stir and add the stock. Then return the shanks to the pot. Bring up to a simmer, cover, then transfer to the oven and cook for 90 minutes and take out of the oven to turn the lamb. Return to the oven and cook for a further 90 minutes.

4: Remove the lid and take out the shanks and skim off any excess fat from the top of sauce. Return the shanks to the sauce and put back into the oven, without the lid, for another 60 minutes. As it cooks the sauce will reduce. When the lamb is tender take it from the oven, replace the lid and set aside for the lamb to rest for 30 mins.

5: Whilst the lamb rests, put your basmati rice in a saucepan and add a tin of coconut milk, fill the tin with tap water and add the water to the saucepan. Bring the rice to the boil, give it a stir and put the lid on, turn the heat down to minimum and cook for 25 minutes.

Recipe Tip

The salmon is delicious served with boiled rice and with stir fried vegetables or alternatively allow to cool and serve with a green salad.

Ginger and Garlic Pan-Fried Salmon Fillet

- Rafael Pittman, Conservatives Abroad Regional Coordinator -

15-30 minutes

2 people

Ingredients:

2 salmon fillets

1 tbsp fresh ginger

2 cloves of garlic

2 tsp soya sauce

1 tbsp white wine (medium dry)

2 tbsp olive oil

½ tsp chilli powder

Jar of tomato sauce or crushed tomatoes

1 green chilli

Method:

1: Pre-heat a frying pan, pour in the olive oil and add all the chopped ginger and garlic and stir until sizzling. Then reduce the heat to add both salmon fillets and fry for about eight minutes turning each side at intervals.

2: If using chilli powder coat the fillets on each side or add one chopped chilli with seeds removed with the garlic and ginger.

3: Halfway through cooking add the white wine and soya sauce.

Trinidad Chicken Stew

- Rupert Matthews, Police and Crime Commissioner for Leicestershire -

1
hour

2-4
people

Ingredients:

1 whole chicken, cut into pieces

1 tsp crushed chillies

1 finely chopped garlic clove

½ tsp black pepper

125ml coconut milk

15g butter

1 tbsp vegetable oil plus 250ml water

3 tbsp chopped spring onions

3 tbsp chopped coriander

4 tbsp dark brown soft sugar

2 tbsp ketchup

1 tsp salt

Method:

1: Place the chicken pieces, onion, crushed chillies, garlic, black pepper, and coconut milk in a bowl. Cover with cling film and allow to stand for a minimum of 30 minutes, preferably for more than an hour.

2: Fry marinated chicken pieces in butter until the chicken is 'browned'.

3: Add the marinade and water, gently bring to the boil.

4: Add half the spring onions and half the coriander, all the sugar and ketchup.

5: Simmer for 20 minutes. Add salt to taste. Serve on a bed of rice with the chopped coriander and spring onion scattered on top.

Recipe Tips

Breadcrumbs – although you can use brown, the white breadcrumbs look better in the mousse. Personally, I prefer to lightly toast the bread before blitzing.

When removing chicken from the simmering water, use a pair of tongs to remove and there will be a certain amount of water as you unwrap the chicken so have kitchen roll or a tea towel available.

Chicken Breasts Stuffed with Chicken Mousse

- Stephen Hammond MP, Wimbledon -

1 hour **8 people**

Ingredients:

8 chicken breasts
2 chicken thighs boned and skinned
1 egg white
2 slices of streaky bacon or pancetta sliced
200ml crème fraîche
50g fresh white breadcrumbs
1 shallot finely chopped
60g butter

As below for sauce

60g butter
1/2 shallots finely chopped
100g mushrooms finely sliced
150ml white wine
500ml chicken stock
350ml double cream

Method:

1: This dish involves flattening the breast, putting the mousse in the middle of breast and the then rolling the breast and poaching.

2: To flatten the breast, take two large pieces of greaseproof / non-stick paper or baking parchment. Put the breast between them and using a rolling pin beat the breast to flatten it. It should at least double in size and the thickness should be no more than say a one-pound coin. Repeat these seven more times and cover the breast with clingfilm and pop in the fridge whilst you make the stuffing.

3: To make the mousse, melt the butter and sweat the shallot until soft (hint this always takes longer than recipe books say, so do allow 3-5 mins). Take your chicken thigh, chop it into cubes and then grind in a blender/ food processor.

As the chicken starts to grind add in the sliced bacon/ pancetta. Then take your sweated shallot and egg white and add them to the chicken. Blend the mixture until it is smooth. The next part is dull to do but worth it. Put enough ice into a large bowl and then put a smaller bowl inside to create an ice bath (the best result is obtained if the smaller bowl has been in the ice bath for five minutes). Take the smoothed chicken mixture and put it into the smaller bowl. Then slowly stir in the crème fraîche and the breadcrumbs. Lightly season to taste.

Chicken Breasts Stuffed with Chicken Mousse

– Stephen Hammond MP, Wimbledon –

4: To stuff the breast. Take the flattened breast from the fridge. Fill the breast with enough stuffing so that the breast can be rolled. The two techniques here are either to put the mousse at one end and roll or to place in the middle and bring the two ends over it. Be careful not to overfill. The result should be sausage like.

Carefully place the filled breast on a square of foil, then roll the foil around the breast and then tighten each end so that they are watertight parcels. Once all the parcels are made, pop in the fridge until ready to poach. This stage can be done up to 12 hours in advance.

5: To cook your chicken. Bring a large pan of water to the boil, turn down so it is simmering and then add your chicken parcel. Poach the parcels for 18-20 mins.

6: Whilst your chicken is poaching, make the sauce. Sweat the chopped shallot and mushrooms in the butter. After softening add 75 ml of wine and reduce by half. Then pour in the stock and bring back to the boil and again reduce until thickened. Then take off the heat and if you want a smooth sauce – strain the mixture through a sieve. I prefer the sauce to have the shallot and mushroom left in. Now add the cream and bring to a thickened consistency.

7: To serve. Remove your chicken parcel from the simmering water. Then unwrap the parcel, slice the breast into 4 or 5 pieces, spoon over the sauce to cover. This is best served with some potato dauphinoise and green vegetables.

One of my favourite ways to spend a day is messing about on the water off the Cornish coast and finish by catching some fish and then landing on a beach you can only access from the water for a BBQ. You just cannot beat fresh fish, cooked and eaten within minutes of being caught whilst watching the sun set.

Mackerel is the fish caught most frequently. Pairing fresh mackerel with beetroot and horseradish is a match made in heaven so I wanted to include this very simple dish as my contribution to this collection of recipes. You don't have to cook and eat it on a beach but I highly recommend it if you can.

Fresh Barbecued Mackerel, Beetroot Salsa and Horseradish Mayo

- Steve Double MP, St Austell and Newquay -

5–10 minutes

4 people

Beetroot salsa

Chop six good sized cooked beetroot

Chop four spring onions

Finely chopped one red chilli (remove the seeds if you don't like it too spicy)

Fresh mint finely chopped – a good handful

Juice of one freshly squeezed lemon

A good glug of olive oil

Mix together and season to taste. Set aside.

Horseradish Mayo

Mix good quality mayonnaise with horseradish – I like it about 50/50 but adjust to your own taste

Method:

1. Gut four large mackerel – or whatever size you have caught (or purchased).

2. Squeeze a little fresh lemon over them and season with salt and pepper.

3. Place on the hot BBQ.

4. Cook for around 5 minutes each side, turning carefully so they do not break up.

5. The fish is cooked when the flesh will easily fall off the bones.

6. Serve fish immediately with a wedge of lemon, the beetroot salsa, a hunk of fresh bread and the horseradish mayo, not forgetting the glass of white (Cornish) wine.

Here at home on Anglesey with Violet my cocker spaniel!

Anglesey Eggs combine amazing Welsh ingredients to produce a perfect vegetarian meal or a side to go with meats. We use ingredients from Anglesey but you can substitute your own.

Virginia sausages are chicken, apricot and herb sausages, produced by Anglesey Fine Foods in Valley, and created in honour of Virginia Crosbie MP's mention of the Farmers Union of Wales Farmhouse Breakfast Week campaign in DEFRA oral questions in the House of Commons. Virginia raised a few smiles by asking the Minister whether she thought a Welsh sausage was the perfect addition to a hearty breakfast.

This recipe serves four as a main course or six as a side.

Anglesey Eggs and Virginia Sausages

- Virginia Crosbie MP, Ynys Môn -

30-45 minutes

4-6 people

Ingredients:

8 hard boiled Welsh eggs (shelled and quartered)

1 large or 2 small Welsh leeks (trimmed and finely diced)

75g Welsh Farmhouse butter

150g Caerphilly or Welsh Farmhouse Cheddar cheese (crumbled)

1kg good quality Welsh potatoes for mashing, peeled and cut into small chunks (or use leftover mash)

630ml Welsh full cream milk

Halen Môn salt

Pepper to taste

50g plain flour

50g fresh breadcrumbs

Virginia Sausages

Method:

1. Pre-heat oven to 200°C, Fan 180°C, Gas 6. Grease a baking dish with butter.

2. Boil potatoes in salted water for about 10 minutes (they should be soft but still hold their shape).

3. Fry the finely diced leeks in 25g of butter until soft.

4. When the potatoes are cooked, drain them and mash with 25g butter and 2 tablespoons of milk. Add the cooked leeks to the mashed potatoes and mix.

5. Spoon the potato mixture into the baking dish and arrange the quartered hard-boiled eggs on top.

6. Beat/whisk together 600ml milk with the flour and butter over a medium heat until the sauce thickens. Simmer for a couple of minutes then add half the cheese and season with salt and pepper. Stir well. Pour sauce over mash and eggs in the dish.

7. Mix the remaining cheese with the breadcrumbs and sprinkle over the mash, eggs, and sauce.

8. Bake for 15-20 mins until cheese is melted and dish is bubbling and golden brown.

Ingredients:
½ cup porridge oats
¼ cup plain flour
¼ cup whole wheat flour
1 tsp quick rising yeast
1 tsp baking powder or
bicarbonate of soda
½ cup milk
½ cup water
Pinch of salt

My contribution is the great Staffordshire Oatcake, in honour of Cannock Chase but also because they are delicious. I normally cook mine in a big slab of butter, and tuck in with some bacon and baked beans, but if you like eggs then a fried one on top is a great addition (I'm told!). My recipe is a bit slap-dash, but they seem to come right every time. This recipe makes two generous oatcakes, or four smaller ones.

Staffordshire Oatcakes

The Rt Hon. Amanda Milling MP, Cannock Chase -

**Just over
an hour**

**2-4
people**

Method:

1: Blitz the oats in a food processor, and then combine all the dry ingredients, while you warm up the milk and water in a microwave or saucepan.

2: Combine the warm (not hot) milk and water with the dry ingredients well, cover and let it stand for about an hour so the yeast can activate and bubble. I sometimes add a bit of extra baking powder or bicarbonate of soda when I can't bring myself to wait that long.

3: I put my bacon and beans on to cook just before I start cooking my oatcakes, so that everything is piping hot and ready at the same time.

4: Then for the oatcakes, melt butter in a piping hot frying pan, ensuring the base of the pan is completely covered so the mixture does not stick.

5: If the batter is not runny enough, just add a little more milk so that it can spread out nicely in the frying pan when dolloped in. Put a healthy spoonful of batter into the hot butter and thinly spread around the pan.

6: Cook as you would a pancake but keeping the oatcakes a little thicker and giving the oatcakes a little longer on each side, so they brown and cook through properly.

7: Be careful when you flip them over, as they are more prone to breaking than pancakes.

8: When cooked through, slide onto a plate with your bacon and beans, or eggs and mushrooms, or cover it in grated cheddar cheese, or all of the above and tuck in!

This is a very quick, easy, and cheap dish which has been a go-to during my time at university. The option to keep extra portions in the fridge to use throughout the week not only means that I have been able to keep costs down but also that meal-prep quickly fits around my busy schedule. This is a very versatile dish; for families, it may work better as a side to a more substantial meal, however, as a student, this is the perfect mid-week meal.

Curried Chicken and Rice

- Callum Murphy, Young Conservatives -

30 minutes

4 people

Ingredients:

200g brown rice

200g sweetcorn

1 large handful frozen peas

1/2 diced onion

About 12cm cucumber, diced

1 cooked chicken breast, cut into small pieces (can be removed for a vegetarian option)

1 tsp medium curry powder (or to taste)

2 tbsp natural yogurt (or to taste)

Bunch of coriander, chopped

Method:

1. Boil the rice.
2. Add peas and sweetcorn to the boiling rice 5 minutes before it is due to be done.
3. Drain the rice and vegetables and run under cold water to cool.
4. Allow to dry.
5. Add onion, cucumber, coriander, and meat (if using).
6. Stir well.
7. Add curry powder and yoghurt.
8. Stir well.

Sweet Tooth

Go on, indulge your sweet tooth.
We've got recipes for cupcakes,
pancakes, and just plain cakes!
Moderation is a virtue, of course —
but isn't cake a virtue too?

These cupcakes hold a special place in my memory and a very special place in my heart, and they are the sweet delight I make to celebrate my grandmother's memory and her life as a voluntary carer. They are straight from the recipe collection my grandmother, Granny Phapha, kept in her mind and shared with all her children, grandchildren and great-grandchildren over the last 90 years.

Back the Blue-Berry Cupcake

- Bently Creswell, Conservative Student -

30 minutes

2-4 people

Ingredients:

4 large eggs

225g self-raising flour

225g butter

225g caster sugar

A splash of vanilla extract

1 tsp of baking powder

A pinch of salt

A handful of blueberries

1 tub of double cream

2 tsp of icing sugar

Method:

1: Soften your butter in a large bowl with the caster sugar, sieving the caster sugar before mixing.

2: To that mixture, add the four eggs, and beat well for 2 minutes, adding a splash of vanilla extract.

3: Add the flour and half a teaspoon of baking powder, sieving them first, and whisk for 3 minutes by electric whisk or 5 minutes by hand.

4: Add a pinch of salt.

5: Once all mixed together, spoon (preferably with a teaspoon) into cupcake cases and submerge your blueberries into the mix.

6: Bake at Fan 150°C 15-20 mins (or till golden brown).

7: Decorating – mix a tub of double cream with two teaspoons of icing sugar, it makes for a lighter and creamier topping than butter icing, and whisk till firm. Dollop the mixture generously onto the cupcakes and spoon out a nest in the cream. Pile the blueberries in the nest.

– Caroline Henry –
Police and Crime Commissioner
for Nottinghamshire

– The Rt Hon. Theresa May MP –
Prime Minister,
July 2016 to July 2017

Just as my mother used
to make them!

Theresa

I first started baking when my husband Darren was serving in the Royal Air Force in the US. It was an escape from the reality of missing my home, family, and friends in my home county of Nottinghamshire. My legendary (in my humble opinion) home-baked scone was born and was an instant hit with our British and American friends. My afternoon teas became an overnight success for those wanting a taste of England across the big pond.

Caroline

Home Baked Scones – two ways!

Scones are a British classic. And just as there's more than one way to pronounce them, there's also more than one way to make them. So will you go with Theresa May's time-honoured take? Or will you go with Caroline Henry's more currant take (pun intended)? If you can't decide, there's an easy way to settle it — try both!

10-15
minutes

2-4
people

Theresa's ingredients:

8oz self-raising flour

1½ oz butter or margarine

1oz castor sugar

1 tbsp milk to bind

Theresa's method:

1: Rub fat into flour. When mixture resembles breadcrumbs stir in sugar. Bind with milk to a dough.

2: Roll out and cut into preferred shape (Best to use a medium pastry cutter).

3: Place on greased baking sheet and cook in a very hot oven for around 8 minutes. You need to keep an eye on them as it is easy to overcook them and make them too dry and flat. They are ready when the top is beginning to colour.

Caroline's ingredients:

8oz self-raising flour

½ tsp salt

1½ oz lard

1 tbsp of sugar

1 egg

A handful of currants

A splash of milk

Caroline's method:

1: Mix the flour and salt. Add and rub in the lard, then mix in the sugar and currants.

2: Mix in the egg and milk to make a dough.

3: Get the oven hot to 180°C and then on grease roof paper trays cut the scones into rounds and place.

4: Use some of the whisked egg to brush the tops.

5: Bake for 10 minutes.

Recipe Tip

Serve hot with a scoop
of two or butterscotch
ice cream.

Rhubarb and Orange Crumble
- The Rt Hon. Damian Green MP, Ashford -

1 hour   4 people

Ingredients:

Filling

4 / 5 medium sticks of rhubarb, washed and cut into chunks

1 / 2 small oranges, removing peel and pith, then slice out the segments' membranes

1½ tsps of powdered ginger

50g runny honey (Kentish is best)

Crumble

175g brown wholemeal flour

75g softened room temperature butter

75g soft brown sugar

Method:

1: Preheat the oven to 200°C, 400°F, Gas 7.

2: Arrange the rhubarb chunks and orange segments into the bottom of a pie dish or two individual dishes. Sprinkle over the powdered ginger and honey.

3: Rub the flour and butter together in a mixing bowl or food processor until the mixture is the consistency of breadcrumbs. Mix in the soft brown sugar then spread the crumble mixture over the rhubarb and orange, pressing down gently.

4: Bake for approximately 30 minutes for one large dish or 20 minutes for 2 individual dishes. Check the filling is bubbling up with pinkish juice at the edges of the crumble and that the topping is browning. (Slightly overcooking makes it more syrupy and delicious).

The first time I remember having these pancakes was in Brighton with my wife when we were celebrating our first wedding anniversary. As a result, every time I have them it brings back fond memories as well as tasting wonderful.

Blueberry Pancakes

- Gagan Mohindra MP, South West Hertfordshire -

5
minutes

2-4
people

Ingredients:

1 pancake mix
A handful of blueberries
A splash of crème fraîche
A splash of maple syrup

Method:

1: Stir in all ingredients together (apart from the blueberries). Once combined, make a well in the centre and add the blueberries. Use a metal spoon to stir until just combined.

2: Heat a large non-stick frying pan over medium-high heat. Grease with butter. Pour three 60ml (1/4 cup) portions of batter into the pan. Cook for 1-2 minutes or until bubbles appear on the surface. Turn and cook for 30 seconds or until cooked through. Transfer to a plate. Cover with foil to keep warm. Repeat, in 3 more batches, with remaining batter to make 9 more pancakes.

Christmas Pudding

- The Rt Hon. Sir John Redwood MP, Wokingham -

5 hours

2-4 people

A seasonal favourite of mine when I make puddings for my family.

Ingredients:

250g wholemeal breadcrumbs –
allow bread to dry out

1 carrot – grated

1 grated orange rind

100g raisins

100g currants

250g sultanas

125g dark brown sugar

125g margarine

1 tbsp milk

1 tbsp brandy

1 tsp ginger

1 tsp mixed spice

1 tbsp syrup

Method:

1: Begin by mixing both the margarine and syrup together in a large mixing bowl.

2: Once smooth, add the other ingredients (using all in one method) and stir vigorously. Once banded together leave to sit for one hour.

3: Once mixture has been left for 1 hour, begin steaming for 4 hours.

Recipe Tip

For tips on steaming see page 113!

Knocking Up Cake

- Katy Bourne OBE, Police and Crime Commissioner for Sussex -

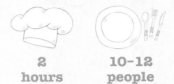

2 hours

10-12 people

Ingredients:

225g butter

225g caster sugar

4 large eggs

225g self-raising flour

500g mixed dried fruits

50g dried apricots

Halved walnut for topping

Method:

1: Preheat the oven to 160°C, 325°F, Fan 140°C, Gas 3.

2: Cut a length of baking parchment (approx. 22 inches) and line a 20cm (8in) spring-form or deep, loose-bottomed round cake tin with it. Don't worry if the sides of the parchment paper crease up as this gives the cake edge a great look and texture.

3: In a large bowl, cream the butter and sugar with an electric mixer or wooden spoon until fluffy, then add the eggs a little at a time, beating well between each addition to prevent curdling.

4: Fold in the flour and beat until all the ingredients are thoroughly mixed. Gently fold the dried fruit into the mixture, stirring with a wooden spoon until well combined.

5: Spoon the mixture into the tin and level the top. If you like, place the halved walnuts on the surface.

6: Put the tin into the oven and bake for 1 ½ to 2 hours. Test the cake for 'doneness' by using a skewer. If the skewer comes out wet and sticky, return the cake to the oven to cook further. When the cake is done, remove from the oven and leave to cool in the tin. Perfect with a cup of tea once you've finished knocking up.

Lemon Drizzle Cake

- Mike Freer MP, Finchley and Golders Green -

1 hour

4 people

Ingredients:

For the cake
225g unsalted butter
225g caster sugar
4 eggs
225g self-raising flour
1 zested lemon

For the drizzle
1½ lemons, juiced
85g caster sugar

Method:

1: Heat the oven to 180°C, Fan 160°C, Gas 4.

2: Beat the softened butter and caster sugar together until creamy, add the eggs (one at a time), slowly mixing in.

3: Sift in the self-raising flour and add in the lemon zest. Mix.

4: Line a loaf tin (8x21cm) with greaseproof paper, spoon in the mixture and level the top with a spoon or spatula.

5: Bake for 45/50 mins. Use a thin skewer to check that it has baked. When it comes out clean, it's done.

6: Allow the cake to cool in the tin. Whilst the cake is cooling, mix the lemon juice and the caster sugar to make the drizzle.

7: Prick the warm cake with the skewer or a fork and dribble the drizzle over the cake. The juice will sink into the cake and provide a lemony, sugary coating on the top.

Chocolate Cake

- Nadine Dorries MP, Mid Bedfordshire -

45 minutes

2-4 people

Ingredients:

For the sponge

225g unsalted butter, plus extra for greasing

225g caster sugar, plus extra for sprinkling

4 free range eggs

220g self-raising flour

2 tsp baking powder

50g cocoa powder

Splash of milk

For the buttercream

100g chopped milk chocolate chopped

200g butter

400g icing sugar

5 tbsp cocoa powder

Splash of milk

Method:

1: **For the sponge:** Preheat the oven to 180°C, Fan 160°C, Gas 4. In a bowl, beat together the butter and sugar. Add all the remaining sponge ingredients and beat together until well combined.

2: Grease and line two 20cm cake tins.

3: Divide the mixture evenly between the cake tins.

4: Bake for 20-25 minutes or until an inserted skewer comes out clean. Cool for a few minutes and pop out onto a cooling rack.

5: **For the buttercream:** Melt the chocolate in the microwave in 30 second bursts.

6: Beat together the butter and icing sugar.

7: Sift in the cocoa powder and add the melted chocolate. Add a splash of milk if too thick.

8: **To assemble:** Spread half the buttercream on the top of one cake, and sandwich the other on top. Spread the rest of the buttercream on top. Alternatively, make half of the buttercream mixture and just melt some chocolate of your choice to pour over the top!

My Mum loved Sherry trifle and whenever there was a family gathering a sherry trifle was always knocked up. The tradition continues each Christmas with my brother and I competing to see who can improve on the recipe, but we always come back to the original.

Sherry Trifle

- Peter Gibson MP, Darlington -

15-30 minutes

4 people

Ingredients:

1 packet of Ladyfinger or Boudoir biscuits

1 jar of strawberry jam

Sherry as much as preference

1 carton custard

2 pint cartons double cream

A handful flaked almonds

A handful Maraschino cherries

Method:

1: Empty the jam into a saucepan and warm over a gentle heat to soften the jam. Drop each biscuit into the jam to fully coat and arrange in the bottom of a deep trifle dish.

2: Once all your biscuits are coated, place in the dish and liberally pour in the sherry to your liking. The sponge soaks it all up so do not worry if you over pour. Add custard to the trifle and leave in fridge preferably overnight to soak and set.

3: Shortly before serving whip the double cream and apply to the top of the trifle and decorate with flaked almonds and cherries.

- Felicity Buchan MP -
Kensington

This is a recipe I would make with my grandmother after she had picked me up from primary school as an afternoon treat. I would make it from the age of 5 (under supervision and not handling the oven myself!). It's simple and quick and requires minimal ingredients. The shortbread can be eaten warm or cold (and stored easily in an airtight container).

- Sam Halliday -
Conservative Student

On the campaign trail early in the morning delivering leaflets in the pouring rain and getting soaked in the process, there is nothing you crave more than a sugary pick-me-up to keep you pushing through. Even after a towel dry and a change of clothes in the back of the car because of the Great British weather, this shortbread is enough for you to want to keep running and pushing leaflets through letterboxes. Proper campaign fuel!

Shortbread – two ways!

There are few treats more comforting than shortbread. And whether you've just come in from a rainy day of campaigning like Sam, or whether you're baking as an after-school treat like Felicity, one thing's for certain — you can't go wrong with shortbread!

40-50 minutes   **3-6 people**

Felicity's ingredients:
255g plain flour
170g butter
85g caster sugar

Sam's ingredients:
335g plain flour
225g butter or margarine
115g caster sugar

Felicity's method:

1: Pre heat the oven to 150°C, Fan 130°C. Sift the flour. Beat the butter (which should be at room temperature) until soft. Beat the sugar into the butter. Fold the flour into the mixture.

2: Transfer the mixture onto a board sprinkled with caster sugar. Use a rolling pin also sprinkled with sugar to roll out the mixture to 5mm thick (½cm). Use pastry cutters to cut the biscuits out. Use a fork to prick the biscuits.

3: Lightly butter a baking tray. Transfer the biscuits onto the baking tray. Put into the oven on a medium/high shelf. Cook for 30 minutes or until golden brown. Allow the biscuits to cool slightly. If desired, they can be sprinkled with caster sugar.

Sam's method:

1: Cream the butter and sugar until soft, (Microwave can help for 20 seconds) then slowly sieve the flour and add small amounts at a time.

2: Mix with a spoon and your hands until the mixture is in a ball.

3: Divide the mixture into 2 pieces and place on baking trays.

4: Roll into identical circles in the middle of the trays, about an inch thick consistently.

5: Prick the tops gently with a fork all the way round, then sprinkle sugar on top.

6: Place in the oven on 170°C, Fan 150°C, Gas 5 for approximately 40 minutes.

7: Cut into shape and eat quickly to avoid them being stolen!

Ingredients:

Sticky Toffee Cake
400g dates
480ml of tea, black and fairly weak
200g light muscovado sugar
50g dark muscovado sugar
2 tbsp golden syrup
4 large eggs
200g unsalted butter, melted
3 tsp mixed spice, heaped
A splash of vanilla extract
350g self-raising flour
2 tsp bicarbonate soda
1 pinch of salt

Sticky Toffee Sauce
100g light muscovado sugar
50g dark muscovado sugar,
or more light
30g butter
2 tbsp golden syrup
A splash of vanilla extract
1 pinch of salt
125ml double cream,
or condensed milk

Buttercream
200g unsalted butter, soft
400g icing sugar
1 dash of milk if needed

Sticky Toffee Cake

- The Rt Hon. Stuart Andrew MP, Pudsey -

**45 minutes
to 1 hour**

**4-6
people**

Method:

1: Preheat the oven to 180°C, Gas 4. Grease and line two 9-inch sandwich tins.

2: To make the cake, place the dates in a saucepan with the tea and bring to the boil, then turn the heat down and leave to simmer for 5 minutes. You can, if you wish, blitz the dates and tea in a blender at this stage, for a smoother texture to your final cake, but it's by no means essential.

3: Whisk the eggs, sugars and syrup together until pale and fluffy. Gradually whisk in the melted butter. Fold in the dates and vanilla. Sift all the dry ingredients over the top of the wet and fold together with a large metal spoon. Be careful not to knock the air out of the mixture.

4: Divide between the two tins and pop into the oven for around 35-40 minutes, or until an inserted skewer comes out clean.

5: While the cake is baking, make the toffee sauce. Place all the ingredients, except for the cream, into a saucepan and stir over a gentle heat until all the sugar has dissolved. Bring to a rolling boil, before stirring in the cream.

7: To make the buttercream, simply whisk the butter until creamy and sift over and whisk in half of the icing sugar, before doing the same again with the second half (this stops it flying out of your bowl and covering your kitchen in icing sugar).

8: Add the rest of the cold toffee sauce, reserving a couple of spoons' worth to drizzle over the top, and whisk in. If the buttercream is too stiff, whisk in a little milk to slacken it slightly.

9: Sandwich the cakes together with half of the buttercream and spread the remaining on the top, before drizzling over the reserved toffee sauce.

Cornish Flat Biscuits

- Scott Mann MP, North Cornwall -

30 minutes

2-4 people

Ingredients:

300g self-raising flour
150g caster sugar
150g margarine
150g any dried fruit
1 medium egg
½ tsp vanilla essence
A splash of milk

Method:

1: Add flour to a mixing bowl (no sieving, we Cornish lob it in). Add margarine. Mix with fingers to breadcrumb texture, getting air in the mixture. Add sugar (chuck it in the middle). Mix again and add the dried fruit and continue mixing.

2: Now add the egg and a splash of milk if required to bring mixture to dough (steady or you will need more flour).

3: Preheat oven to 180°C. Now flour the worktop and roll to ½ inch thick. Use the flour cutter to shape into separate biscuits – then line the baking tray and bake for 12–15 minutes until golden.

My grandparents both originated in the Vale of Evesham from horticulturist backgrounds. When they bought a farm near Banbury it seemed natural to them to plant orchards. We still grow apples and pears at home today and make our own cider on Apple Day in October.

Cider Cake

- Victoria Prentis MP, Banbury -

1 hour

4 people, recipe can be doubled

Ingredients:

150ml cider

225g sultanas

120g butter

120g light soft brown sugar

2 eggs

1 tsp bicarbonate of soda

225g flour

Method:

1: Soak the sultanas in cider overnight and stir lightly.

2: Cream the butter and sugar together.

3: Add the eggs and half of the flour.

4: Add the bicarb and fruit and cider mixture.

5: Add the rest of the flour.

6: Cook in a greased and lined 18cm square cake tin at 180°C for about an hour.

7: Check and cover if top burning.

8: Leave in tin to cool before serving.

Recipe Tip

Cool in the tin for at least 30 minutes, turn out onto a wire rack and dust with icing sugar.

Colchester Gingerbread Cake

- Will Quince MP, Colchester -

1 hour

2-4 people

Ingredients:

100g margarine or unsalted cooking butter

100g golden syrup

100g dark syrup / black treacle

75g caster sugar

150ml milk

1 tbsp orange marmalade

100g plain flour

100g self-raising flour

1tsp ginger

1tsp mixed spice

1 tsp orange essence

1 tsp candied ginger or crystallised ginger finely chopped

½ tsp bicarbonate soda

2 eggs

1 sachet icing sugar

Method:

1: Pre-heat the oven to 190°C, Fan 170°C, Gas 5.

2: Line a circa 30x20cm/12x8in tin with baking parchment.

3: In a saucepan, gently melt the margarine, golden syrup, dark syrup/ black treacle, caster sugar, milk, and orange marmalade.

4: In a bowl, mix the plain flour, self-raising flour, ginger, mixed spice, bicarbonate of soda.

5: Once melted, pour the contents of the saucepan over the dry ingredients, and add the beaten eggs.

6: Add the finely chopped candied or crystallised ginger and the orange essence.

7: Mix well until smooth.

8: Pour into the prepared tin and bake for 45-55 minutes.

Jammy Steamed Sponge

- The Rt Hon. Oliver Dowden CBE MP, Hertsmere -

3 hours   6--8 people

Ingredients:

For the sponge

175g very soft unsalted butter, plus more for greasing

175g self-raising flour

175g caster sugar

3 large eggs

1 tbsp juice of ½ lemon

For the topping

250g jam

1 tbsp juice of ½ lemon

Method:

1: Put the butter, flour, sugar, eggs and lemon juice in a food processor and whizz together. Add a little milk if the mix is too thick. It should be a thick, pouring consistency.

2: Butter the pudding basin and pudding basin lid. Put the jam in the pudding basin and mix in the lemon juice. Pour the sponge mixture on top of the jam and put on the lid.

3: Pour boiling water into a large, lidded saucepan. Place the pudding basin in the saucepan. The water should come about half to two-thirds of the way up the side of the pudding basin. Put the lid on the saucepan.

4: Put the saucepan on a low heat. The pan should keep boiling, with the lid on. The saucepan should not boil dry. If necessary, top up with more boiling water.

5: Let the pudding steam for a minimum of 2 hours. When it's ready, lift it out carefully and let rest for a couple of minutes. Then turn it out onto a large plate.

6: Serve with cream, ice cream or custard.

Waste Not, Want Not

The Rt Hon. The Baroness Jenkin of Kennington

When it comes to waste, Anne Jenkin runs a three-line whip. The Conservative peer is a prominent campaigner against food waste, so we asked Anne to take us through her daily menu and tell us how she manages to save food...

I have always been frugal. I think in a former life I must have been a war baby! I enjoy taking those little pots of leftovers at the back of the fridge and turning them into something delicious.

But in recent years, as we have all learned more about the environmental costs of food waste, I have become increasingly keen to eat and shop sustainably.

The earth's resources are finite. But we don't always act like it. Believe it or not, if food waste were a country it would be the third-biggest emitter of CO_2 in the world, coming straight after the USA and China. I believe we all can do more to waste less.

My cooking style is based on this principle. If we are all a bit more careful with our shopping and cooking, we can learn to live very well — and save a bit of money in the process!

Here is a typical daily menu in the Jenkin household.

Breakfast

My husband and I like porridge for breakfast, but we both want it prepared in completely different ways. If you like both, you could mix and match and create a third!

Anne's Soaked Oats

If you shop wisely, porridge oats are still 75p a kilo. Soak a handful of them overnight in either milk or plant-based milk. I prefer unsweetened soya or almond. In the morning, add a dollop of either berries or stewed fruit (I fill the freezer with garden raspberries/gooseberries/apples/rhubarb to see me through the winter), a splash of soya yoghurt and a small handful of nuts and seeds. Bingo — healthy, sustaining and delicious! No cooking and only the bowl to wash up.

Waste Not, Want Not

Bernard's Cooked Porridge

The trick to this is real oatmeal rather than porridge oats. Again, soak a good handful overnight in water: this speeds up cooking in the morning. Bring the pan to the boil and then turn off the heat entirely. It will be cooked by the time you've made a coffee. My husband normally adds fruit, usually stewed fruit or berries, but of course this is optional.

Lunch

During lockdown I cooked soup for six of us almost every single day. Healthy, cheap, delicious and a great way to use up leftovers — not to mention the bits of vegetable you find at the bottom of the fridge. These vegetables are often past their prime, but you can still use most of them! Things like broccoli stalks, outer cabbage leaves and core are great for soups.

Use real stock if you have it (from boiling a ham or chicken bones). If not, add a stock cube for taste. Throw in a good dollop of lentils and whatever vegetables you have to hand: parsnip, carrot, potato, onion.

Remember that celeriac, sweet potato and swedes all last for ages and that a small chunk goes a long way.

Season it with anything leftover you have to hand: mashed potatoes, pasta, rice. I mash it all because we like a chunky consistency, but blend if you prefer a smooth texture.

Waste Not, Want Not

Dinner

Quick, Easy and Tasty Fish Pie

Frozen supermarket fish are perfect if you're on a budget. But be sure to check they come from a sustainable source. Start with a layer of thawed frozen spinach. Add a layer of defrosted fish fillets. Then top with a layer crème fraîche mixed with either mustard or pesto, depending on taste. Add a covering of breadcrumbs and grated cheese made from ends of loaves, and leftover heels of cheese, grated and put in freezer for just this occasion. And that's it! Put it in the oven until bubbling.

Daal

My family love daal. It's cheaper than chips — and much healthier too!

I tend to make it differently every time, but the trick is in the spices. I usually use yellow split peas, soaked overnight, but lentils are fine. Many recipes tell you to fry the onions and spices, but that's more calories and washing up, so I just use the one pot.

Put everything in a saucepan and boil it with a stock cube, a chopped-up onion, a good squeeze of tomato puree, a vegetable of some kind to bulk it out – butternut squash is perfect – and then add spices. Garlic and fresh grated ginger are crucial, but you can also add a combination of anything else you might have in the store cupboard: chilli (fresh, dried or powder), curry powder, garam masala, cumin, or whatever you have to hand.

Boil until everything is thoroughly cooked. Add a tin of tomatoes and stir it in. Taste it — but beware of spices. I usually think it isn't spicy enough, until a few seconds later when I find that it is!

At the end stir in two of three lumps of frozen spinach. Serve with brown rice and some naan bread.

This is approximately 40p a portion, tasty and filling.

Recipes reprinted by kind permission of Jean Jones whose husband Peter (pictured with Lady Thatcher) compiled, edited and published the original 'The Conservative Celebrity Recipe & Cook Book' on behalf of the Darlington Conservatives in 1988.

Cooking Up Some History

It's time to reheat a few old dishes. In this section, we've reprinted some of the classic recipes from a Conservative Party cookbook, published in 1988. From Mr Denis Thatcher's favourite Salmon Fish Cakes to Ted Heath's Pumpkin Pie, you can't go wrong with the oldies.

Cold Curried Chicken with Grapes

– Mrs. Angela C. R. Rumbold, Mitcham and Morden –

Ingredients:

4 chicken breasts

2 cubes chicken stock (made in ½ pt boiling water)

1 large onion

2 tbsps curry powder

1 tbsp plain flour

Oil

Pepper

Salt

½ lb green grapes

¼ pt single cream

Method:

1: Cover the bottom of a heavy saucepan with oil and heat.

2: Slice onions and cook until soft.

3: Add flour and mix into a paste.

4: Add curry powder and mix thoroughly.

5: Pour in stock and add chicken pieces.

6: Cook at oven 4 for ¾ hour.

7: Add cream gently and fully cool.

8: Before serving cut and pip grapes and stir into mixture.

The
Conservative
Celebrity
Recipe & Cook
Book

Compiled, Edited and Published
by
P.J. Jones

Printed by
G-print
6, Tower Road, Darlington, Co. Durham. DL3 6RU.

Copyright © P.J. Jones MCMLXXXVIII
all rights reserved.

Delicious on a summer evening.

Australian Boiled Fruit Cake

- Dame Jill Knight, Birmingham Edgbaston -

Ingredients:

12 oz mixed dried fruit
2 oz chopped walnuts
7 oz white sugar
¼ lb butter
9 oz flour
2 eggs
1 cup water

Method:

1: Put the dried fruit, chopped walnuts, sugar, butter and water in a large saucepan.

2: Bring to the boil, then simmer for 5-10 minutes.

3: Allow to cool for 30-40 minutes then beat in eggs and flour.

4: Add a pinch of salt.

5: Bake in oven for 30 minutes at Mark 4 then 45 minutes at Mark 1.

Quick and Easy Biscuits

- Dame Jill Knight, Birmingham Edgbaston -

Ingredients:

No. 1.
4 oz butter or margarine
½ cup caster sugar
1 level tbsp golden syrup

No. 2.
1 cup self-raising flour
1 cup rolled oats
½ tsp bi-carbonate of soda
To taste almond or vanilla flavouring

Method:

1: Put No. 1. in medium sized saucepan and melt the ingredients slowly.
2: Add No. 2. And mix well.
3: Place in teaspoonfuls on to a well-greased baking tray, leaving room to spread and bake in a moderate oven.
4: Gas Mark 4 for approximately 10-15 minutes, or until golden brown.
5: Leave to cool slightly before removing from the tin.

Lemon Syllabub

- Dame Jill Knight, Birmingham Edgbaston -

Ingredients:

1 lemon

3 – 4 oz caster sugar

¼ pt sweetish Spanish white wine or sherry

½ pt double cream

Method:

1: Grate the rind of one lemon, squeeze and strain the juice.

2: Put both the rind and the juice into a large bowl together with caster sugar, Spanish white wine (or sherry) and double cream.

3: Whisk altogether until the mixture becomes quite thick.

4: Spoon into tall glasses and leave in a cool place.

A great timesaver as a sweet for a dinner or lunch party. It is best made the day before it is to be eaten.

Mrs. Edwina Currie M.P.

◇◆◇◆◇◆◇

Passion Cake

Ingredients:

225g wholemeal flour
15g baking powder
5g cinnamon
185g grated carrot
185g soft margarine
175g soft brown sugar
1 orange for finely grated zest
20 ml fresh orange juice
3 eggs
45g walnuts chopped
40 ml semi skimmed milk

Topping

75g soft margarine
350g low fat soft cheese
75g icing sugar
30g walnut halves

Method:
Mix together flour, baking powder, cinnamon and carrot.
Cream together margarine, sugar, zest and orange juice. Gradually beat in
Add flour mixture and walnuts.
Mix, adding milk for a soft consistency. Divide into lightly greased 23cm t
Bake at 180C / 350F / Gas 4 for 30 minutes until well risen and golden brow

Cream margarine and then mix in cheese and icing sugar.
Sandwich cooled cakes with 2/3 topping. Spread remainder on top an
walnut halves.

Recipe Tip

Edwina says: "These days, as we are now so much more prosperous than in pre-Thatcher times, I would use butter rather than margarine."

Edwina has starred in Channel 4's 'Come Dine With Me' twice. Pictured here being filmed in her kitchen in 2010 with her old dog Sheba offering to help.

Passion Cake

- Mrs. Edwina Currie, South Derbyshire -

45 minutes

8 people

Ingredients:

225g wholemeal flour
15g baking powder
5g cinnamon
185g grated carrot
185g soft margarine
175g soft brown sugar
1 orange (for finely grated zest)
20ml fresh orange juice
3 eggs
45g walnuts (chopped)
40ml semi-skimmed milk
75g soft margarine
350g low fat soft cheese
75g icing sugar
30g walnut halves

Method:

1: Mix together flour, baking powder, cinnamon and carrot.
2: Cream together margarine, sugar, zest and orange juice, gradually beating in the eggs.
3: Add flour mixture and chopped walnuts.
4: Mix, adding milk for a soft consistency.
5: Divide into lightly greased 23cm tins.
6: Bake at 180 °C (350F/Gas 4) for 30 minutes until well risen and golden brown.
7: Cream margarine then mix in cheese and icing sugar.
8: Sandwich cooled cakes with 2/3 toppings. Spread the remainder on top and decorate with walnut halves.

Can be served as cuddle cake without the topping.

Mr. Denis Thatcher's Favourite Salmon Fish Cakes

- The Rt Hon. Mrs. Margaret Thatcher, Finchley -

Ingredients:

16oz tinned Red Salmon
1oz butter
½ lb mashed potato
2 eggs
Salt and pepper
Breadcrumbs

30 minutes

2 people

Method:

1: Remove any skin and bones and chop fish coarsely.

2: Heat the butter in a saucepan, add the fish, potatoes, yolk of one egg, salt and pepper.

3: Stir over heat for a few minutes.

4: When cold, shape into round flat cakes, brush over with beaten egg, coat with breadcrumbs and fry in hot fat.

5: The fish may be made into one large cake instead of several small ones, in which case grease a flat tin and place mixture into same.

6: Brush over with egg, cover with slightly browned breadcrumbs and bake for about 20 minutes in fairly hot oven (Gas 6, 375F).

The Conservative Celebrity Recipe & Cook Book

Compiled, Edited and Published
by
P.J. Jones

◆

Margaret Thatcher

Printed by
G-print
6, Tower Road, Darlington, Co. Durham. DL3 6RU.

Copyright © P.J. Jones MCMLXXXVIII
all rights reserved.

Mother in Law's - Bacon Hot Pot Supper Dish
- Winston S. Churchill, Davyhulme -

**3-4
people**

Ingredients:
1 lb bacon rashers
1 lb potatoes
4 onions
Sage
Pepper to taste
½ pint cold water

Recipe Tip

Serve with fresh or
frozen peas.

Method:
1: Discard rind from bacon and cut
   into small pieces.
2: Into a casserole dish slice
   2 onions.
3: Cover with a layer of bacon pieces
   and sprinkle with sage and a dash
   of pepper.
4: Continue with another layer of
   onions, bacon and sage.
5: Peel and slice potatoes and
   arrange on top.
6: Add ½ pint cold water.
7: Sprinkle a little salt on top of
   potatoes.
8: Bake in oven at 175 °C for
   2 hours.

Pumpkin Pie

- The Rt Hon. Edward Heath, Old Bexley and Sidcup -

Ingredients:

8oz shortcrust pastry

1 lb pumpkin flesh with pith (skin and seeds removed and cut into 1 inch cubes)

½ pt water

2oz apricot, plum or greengage jam

1 egg

1½ tbsp brown sugar

1 tsp ground nutmeg

1oz currants, raisins or sultanas

Serve hot or cold.

Serve the pie accompanied with thick cream.

Method:

1: Boil the pumpkin flesh in the water, stirring occasionally to prevent sticking, for about 10 minutes.

2: Drain and cool.

3: Roll out the pastry and line an 8 inch flan tin or pastry plate. Trim off excess pastry from the edges of the tin or plate and reserve the trimmings.

4: Spread the pastry case with a thin layer of jam.

5: Add the eggs, sugar and most of the nutmeg to the cooled pumpkin flesh and either blend in a food processor, or mash with a fork until smooth.

6: Mix in the dried fruit and pour the mixture into the pastry case.

7: Sprinkle the remaining nutmeg on top of the pie and decorate with a lattice made from the pastry trimmings.

8: Cook in a preheated oven at 200 °C/400F/Gas 6 for 15 minutes, then reduce heat to 180°C/350F/Gas 4 and cook for a further 15 minutes or until the pastry is golden brown.

Index

Index

Savoury

Sweet Tooth

Waste Not, Want Not

Cooking Up Some History

Acknowledgements

To all our recipe and photo contributors - there would be no book without you!

Paul Thatcher, Jean Jones, Peter Gibson.

The compilation team: Paul Place, Beth Mitchell, Simon Phillips, Stephen Ion, Iain Makepeace, Adam Gething, Alexander Cobb, Theo Von Prondzynski, Laura Saunders, Jonathan Burkitt, the CCHQ Field Team, the Paragon team.